The Adventures of

DJ Steve

And

Jackie Jack

Jason Dulac
and
Landon Action

JACKIE
JACK

Bring Your Pet To School Day

It was bring your pet to School Day

And DJ Steve wanted to show everyone he was brave

Because Billy the Bully called him a cat the other day

DJ Steve wanted to show everyone he was Dog brave

But DJ Steve didn't want to bring his dog

Because his little pup wasn't big and Strong

So DJ Steve Knew what he had to do

He pulled out his magic pencil and he drew

He started with a toilet bowl dinosaur

With teeth on the lid that could move mountains when you flush

Which would leave the bully's running in a
rush

Because it was also a triple headed
monster and part bear

No bully's would mess with DJ Steve
because they would definitely be scared

DJ Steve was gonna be the bravest kid in
school

He was gonna be super cool

When he finished drawing his pet came to
life

He called it the super toilet monster king

And he brought it to school

DJ Steve was right, the bully's were
scared and everyone thought he was cool

Later on that day DJ Steve and his pet sat
on the couch

That's when his baby brother Jackie Jack came out and started to shout

Potty...

And chased the pet potty monster out of the house

<u>Clean Up</u>

DJ Steve wanted to go out and play

But DJ Steve had to clean his room today

DJ Steve got it done fast because DJ Steve

Wanted to play soccer in the backyard grass

DJ Steve called mom so he could prove to her he got the job done

But before mom got up the stairs

He saw his little brother Jackie Jack

Mom came in and the room was trashed

She looked at DJ Steve and she was not impressed

DJ Steve was confused

Because he did what mom asked him to
do

Then mom saw in the corner of her eye
Jackie Jack

Running around throwing trash

Mom looked at DJ Steve and they both
laughed

And then they realized Jackie Jack needed
a bath

Soccer game

DJ Steve was mad cause baby Jackie Jack

Was always ruining his plans
Being a big brother was supposed to be
coo

But baby Jackie Jack was always making
him look like a fool.

But today would be different because it
was the Soccer match at school

DJ Steve was the greatest goalie the
School had seen

But unfortunately the other team was
missing a man

This is when DJ Steve had a plan

He volunteered Jackie Jack

Give the other team the baby and his
team would definitely be the champs

But little did DJ Steve know

His baby brother Jackie Jack was a soccer pro

He took out DJ Steve's team alone

While Scoring a thousand goals

Making DJ Steve the worst goalie the School had known

Jackie Jack became a legend though

Monkey Kon

DJ Steve was excited all day

As DJ Steve was about to play the new
Monkey Kon game

But when the time finally came

Mom told him Jackie Jack had to play

DJ Steve didn't want to share with his
brother

But DJ Steve wasn't gonna argue with his
mother

So he grabbed two controllers and they
started to play

But lightning hit the house

And before he knew it

he and his brother were inside the game

But Jackie Jack saw a baby Monkey and
ran off to play

Before DJ Steve could run or shout

the ground it started to shake

and big old Monkey Kon

was standing in front of his face.

DJ Steve started to shake but Monkey
Kon told him not to be afraid

Monkey Kon needed help to catch his
baby brother

And get him home so he didn't get in
trouble with his mother

And DJ Steve needed to get Jackie Jack

So the two teamed up and got their
brothers back

And then lightning hit their house again
and DJ Steve woke up from bed

It was just a dream, it was all in his head

<u>Mouse in the House</u>

DJ Steve's Mom saw a mouse

DJ Steve's Mom ran out of the house.

DJ Steve decided to be brave

He was gonna catch the mouse today

DJ Steve decided to set a trap

He put a piece of cheese on a string

He wanted to have the mouse follow the cheese out of the house

But everything did not go as planned

because Jackie Jack was a hungry man

And thought the cheese was for him

With one bite it was gone

Now everything had gone wrong

But DJ Steve knew what to do

He looked at Jackie Jack and said let's play cat

Jackie Jack got on all fours

And with a meow he chased the mouse out of the house

HesstourAt

Jackie Jack gets into Trouble

Jackie Jack was sad today
  because Jackie Jack got in trouble today

Because he put money into the video
game

And Mom told him that's where you put
the disk into play

But now that the system had been fixed

Jackie Jack went to check on it

While taking his green apple that he had
been eating for a bit

But all of a sudden he bit a seed and spit
it out while saying eweee

But the seed went in the game
And the disk it wouldn't play

Mommy was mad again.

But DJ Steve saw what had gone on and
told mom it was an accident

so getting mad at Jackie Jack was
definitely wrong

So Mom apologized and the day went on

The Missing Magic Pencil

Everything was wrong

DJ Steve's magic pencil was gone

DJ Steve didn't know what to do

Than he saw Jackie Jack and yelled what did you do

Because Jackie Jack was running fast

He drew an oven monster with an evil laugh

Jackie Jack quickly handed DJ Steve his magic Pencil back

DJ Steve had to think quickly as he drew the super toilet monster king

And that is when the fight began of course the super toilet monster king would win

Saving DJ Steve and Jackie Jack

Who were happy to have their friend back

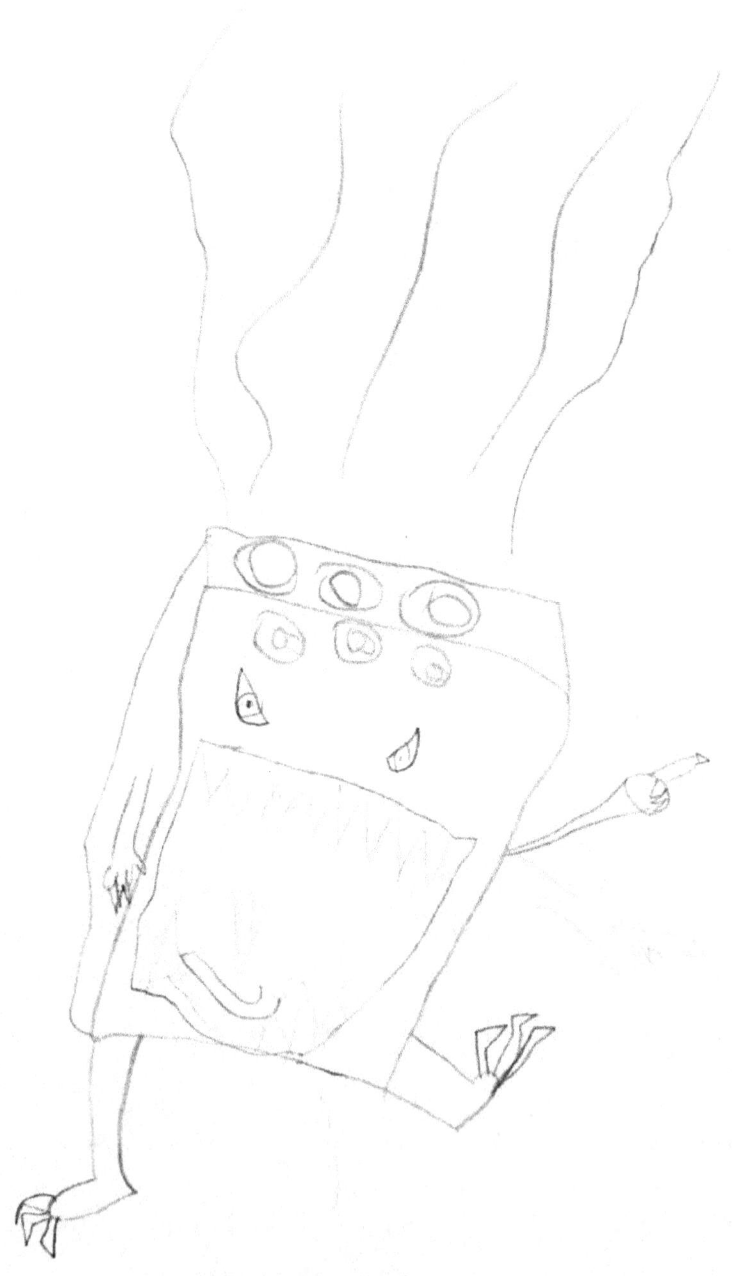

vs

Clown Cheese's Pizzaria

Jackie Jack's birthday was today

So they went to Clown Cheese's Pizzeria to celebrate

Everyone was having fun

But Jackie Jack was a hungry one

That's when clown cheese came out with pizza for them to eat

But before Jackie could have a bite he noticed there was pepperoni on his slice

And pepperoni Jackie Jack did not like

So he quickly threw the slice

Which hit Clown Cheese square in the nose but clown cheese he was ok

He yelled food fight and threw pizzas for the rest of the day

While Jackie Jack and his friends ran
around and played

And DJ Steve he had to clean the mess
they made

As today was his brothers big day

www.ingramcontent.com/pod-product-compliance
Lightning Source LLC
Chambersburg PA
CBHW060925130726
48001CB00006B/2423